My Master Is My Self

My Master Is My Self

The Birth of a Spiritual Teacher

ANDREW COHEN

MOKSHA PRESS

1995

OTHER BOOKS BY ANDREW COHEN

An Unconditional Relationship to Life

Enlightenment Is a Secret

Autobiography of an Awakening

CONTENTS

Editor's Foreword

What follows is the story of an extraordinary meeting. A meeting that occurred beyond time and that revealed a wisdom so deep that it dares even the most open-minded to suspend all ideas about what is real and what is true just to begin to let it in. It is the story of a love so profound that it pierces the illusion of separation and explodes the vast expanse of beginningless and endless freedom that wants only to be discovered by an innocent heart. This is a meeting that is dreamt of but few ever have the good fortune to experience, defying the limits of what most believe possible. Yet the diaries and letters that compose this story attest to the fact that it did indeed occur.

My Master Is My Self chronicles the meeting between Andrew Cohen and his last teacher H. W. L. Poonja, and the events that unfolded in Andrew's life over the three years that followed. An intimate, first-hand account of a profound awakening is rare. And it is even more rare when such an account is articulated in a way that conveys not just the experience itself, but the depth of understanding that arose from it. This is what marks *My Master Is My Self* as such an unusual work. First published in 1989, it has become a modern underground spiritual classic.

INTRODUCTION

Nothing I had previously been involved with prepared me for the remarkable events which are described in this book.

In the early 1970s I began seeking for Enlightenment. I spent eight years in India, meditating, seeing teachers, and reading spiritual books. In 1980 I went to live in England and this search was still the primary focus in my life. After five years, I felt frustrated and returned to India. I had planned on going to meditate but somehow wasn't satisfied with that. There was a longing for something else.

When I met H.W.L. Poonja, a disciple of Sri Ramana Maharshi, I had a sense that my search could actually come to an end. When I met Andrew Cohen that possibility became a reality.

The meeting between Guru and disciple is a mystery. It is a mystery that can only be known by those involved and even then only its intimations can be felt. This book is a detailed account of such a meeting.

I was asked to write a brief narrative to help introduce the material in this book. This appears throughout in italicized print.

Murray Feldman
March 1989

Part One

Diary
March 25 – April 14, 1986

*In December of 1985, while living in southern India,
I was approached by a young American.*

*"Are you Murray Feldman? Can you give me the
address of this teacher you've been with?"*

*He introduced himself as Andrew Cohen. He told me
that recently he had been in England, where he had
learned from a friend of mine that I was spending time
with a great but little-known spiritual teacher. He explained that immediately upon hearing of this teacher, he
knew that he had to meet him. I invited Andrew to my
room and told him about my time with this man, whose
name was Hari Lal Poonja.*

*Poonjaji, a disciple of Sri Ramana Maharshi, was
seventy-five years old. I told Andrew that I had never
met anyone like him, and that he had seemed to me like
a living God. Through being with this man, I had begun
to understand what Ramana Maharshi had meant when
he said that being in the company of a Satguru is the
most important catalyst for Self-Realization. Profoundly
inspired by the time that I had spent with Poonjaji, and
aware that I had not fully understood his teachings, I
knew that I had to see him again.*

*At the end of January 1986, I returned to Lucknow in
northern India to spend more time with Poonjaji.*

*Andrew arrived at the end of March. He told me that
although he had no desire to enter into a formal relationship with a teacher, he felt compelled to meet this man.*

I introduced Andrew to Poonjaji on the morning of March 25th. At this meeting Andrew had a profound realization. After speaking to Poonjaji for only a few minutes he turned to me and said, "I've always been Free!"

Poonjaji had spoken to me often about his desire to find someone who would continue with the teaching after he died. It was at this moment that I knew that Andrew was the one for whom Poonjaji had been waiting.

This book is an account of the meeting between Andrew Cohen and H. W. L. Poonja, and of the events which followed. It is told primarily through a diary which Andrew kept during that period. Also included are the letters exchanged between Andrew and Poonjaji over the next three years.

The following is from the diary Andrew kept during his first three weeks with Poonjaji.

Day One
MARCH 25, 1986

I had my first talk with Sri Poonjaji this morning. We were talking about "effort." He said to me, "You don't have to make any effort to be free." I saw clearly that making constant effort had become a habit. I then understood that making no effort or living effortlessly could also become a habit. In that moment I had a deep and clear experience or glimpse of what making no effort meant. A brief moment of complete freedom. Real insight and understanding of what liberation means. It is so simple, so obvious, and in fact, right here with us all the time. Poonjaji saw this happen and said he saw radiance come over me during this moment. Fascinating. I did understand.

Day Two
MARCH 26, 1986

...Talking more about how "doing anything" just creates more bondage. Adding anything is just more becoming. Just more to do. Anything more only takes us away from where we already are which means only adding and more to let go of. More bondage and illusion of selfhood.

Day Four
MARCH 28, 1986

He showed me a letter written to him by a woman from Brussels whom he met in Rishikesh in 1968. The letter, which she wrote to him recently, described the experience of her enlightenment. Very moving and convincing.

...He told me, "Do not be attached to the teacher and do not be attached to enlightenment." Because this creates separation...Talked about the experience I had on the first day with him and he said that it was very rare.

Day Five
MARCH 29, 1986

Sitting outside the General Post Office. Continue to feel light and happy inside and wonder if it is due to contact with Poonjaji or just that I feel well. Also inwardly feel more and more that there is nothing to hold onto. See the mind constantly reaching out to grasp and see again and again that there is nothing but my own mind searching for and creating objects—concepts—that do not really exist. Again, no security anywhere. This is disturbing me on one level—but at the same time, due to Poonjaji's influence, I don't mind. It all doesn't matter....This creates a gentle tension within. This also doesn't matter....

Is all this (nothing really at all) due to Poonjaji? Is it only myself? Maybe this too doesn't really matter.

In the afternoon we had I think the most fascinating discussion of my entire life! We talked about the ending of time—how in enlightenment one goes beyond time itself. We talked about my experience of timelessness that occurred shortly after I met him. We then talked more about what it means to experience the timeless—how this whole experience of births and deaths over millennia is not real—that at the moment of enlightenment, in one instant, one realizes that none of it ever existed. Like waking up from a dream. Enlightenment is an instant of recognition that cancels out the whole of one's separate existence. The past and all of one's personal history (no matter how long) is burned—the candle flame is blown out and in fact, one realizes that *one never existed.*

Samsara only exists in time. Enlightenment is beyond time. It was never born and can never die. Beyond opposites, beyond comparison—no trinity. This whole world, this existence, is only a dream....

Day Six
MARCH 30, 1986

When I arrived in the morning Poonjaji asked me what time it was. He was surprised to discover that it was 10:40 as he explained that he had been "somewhere" else or in a vacant state for what he was pleased and surprised to discover had been four hours. He said he had been out of his body. He told me he had slept very little and had been thinking all night about our discussions of the evening before. He said that my understanding was very rare, but that he felt a thin veil or "mist" still lay between he and I. He told me that he had to be honest with me—for his own well-being—otherwise he would feel burdened and unclean.

An Indian disciple arrived at 11:30 and we talked together of my experience of emptiness that occurred on the first day. He explained to Poonjaji and me that he too had seen the look on my face and said that he had also felt something at that moment.

During my afternoon break I had the odd sensation of a gentle but very mild pressure existing somewhere inside myself. It was so subtle that I wasn't even sure if it really existed or if it was just my imagination. Ever so slightly uncomfortable…I imagined that this was Poonjaji's influence and that the discomfort was my own fear of letting go.…

In the afternoon Dr. Ganga Singh and his wife were at Poonjaji's when I arrived. Poonjaji immediately began to tell them of my understanding of the night before and of how rare it was.

Went for a walk in the evening with Poonjaji to the park. Walking back to his house he told me how he felt detached—vacant—empty—how he knew he was not his body.

Day Seven
March 31, 1986

…He talked about karma. With Enlightenment the whole karmic balance is "burnt" in an instant. How the past vanishes—how once again it never existed and one continues to live in a state where there is no past and no future. How due to the "momentum" of the past karma we continue to live in this world, but being awake, remain completely free of involvement because we *know* that it is all unreal.

Yesterday morning I spoke with Poonjaji about the "mist" which he had mentioned lay between us. I told him that I thought it was my ego. He agreed. I told him that on one hand he wanted me to be an independent and free person — and that on the other I saw that to pierce this veil I must surrender to him. How to reconcile these two extremes? He was quiet for a long while and then shed tears. He said I had asked a very difficult question. He was silent for a long time and then said, "The Source commands Surrender, and that has nothing to do with personality." He also told me that this question that I had asked had not come from me but had come from the "source."

Day Eight
APRIL 1, 1986

Another fantastic day in this unexpected adventure of seeing into the nature of reality, truth or self. Again and again there is too much coming too fast and I feel I'm losing the ability to capture it all on paper…learning so, so much. Can't really believe it all.

In the morning I told Poonjaji about my experience of cosmic consciousness when I was sixteen years old. I asked him about the difference between this experience, which I felt was a deep experience of "fullness," compared to the Buddhist teaching of "voidness." Were they the same? Were they different experiences? Which was higher? He was very moved by what happened when I was sixteen. He said that I had experienced everything. He said that "nothing was missing" from what I had told him. He said that if anything needed to be added — or that if I had missed something he surely would have told me. He said he was very hard on his students and was being straight with me. He said that the limitless and timeless could not be approached by the conceptual mind. He made clear that this was futile and impossible. That experiences like this were beyond individuality and therefore not to be grasped by the individual mind or understanding. It was futile to compare and judge what was in fact beyond comparison. He pointed out that this experience had happened spontaneously and without effort. That afterwards I had wanted to reattain this experience through effort. He again pointed out the futility of trying to attain something that could not be held in any way. He made clear that instead of me trying to reattain this unattainable unhaveable reality, I should believe in its truth and let go and let it — *grab me* — let it ***envelop me.*** That this is where the question of faith came in.

He then explained how fullness and emptiness were ultimately the same thing, that they had to be. This, though I understood it when he explained it, soon was out of my reach.

Need to probe more deeply into this question of FULLNESS VS. VOIDNESS.

Day Nine
APRIL 2, 1986

This morning spoke with Poonjaji. He was very pleased when I said, "Most people seek great security in a continuous postponement of freedom." He sat up in bed when I said this and he had me repeat it again so he could write it down in his notebook.

Day Ten
April 3, 1986

Morning. We spoke again about fullness and emptiness. He said that there was something beyond fullness and emptiness that witnesses and perceives the fullness and emptiness.

Talked more with Poonjaji about the above in the evening. That which perceives form and emptiness can never be known. That which perceives is in fact only the Self. The Self can only know Itself. That which perceives the reality of the Self within the individual is **only** the Self. It cannot be other than the Self. Hence the impossibility of the separate individual ego to perceive what it cannot contain or grasp. Only the Self can know the Self. That which perceives and that which is perceived are one and the same. This division also is not real. Only the Self is.

How can what is not real and which has no substance know what is real? It is an impossibility! Only the real can know the real!

The Self can only know the Self. The Self is perfect. Nothing can be added to that — for it contains everything. Only the illusion of not knowing this can be removed. Who knows the Self? The Self only! *It cannot be otherwise!*

3:30 P.M. Fantastic insights and talk with Poonjaji this morning. Where is all this coming from? Poonjaji says it is not coming from me but from the Self. ***Trust in that.***

...I understood finally that it is not only this separate ego that is nonexistent — the illusion of this world and the life on it also — but in fact ***the whole universe doesn't exist!*** The universe is Samsara. It has no substance and is unreal.

Creation itself is an illusion.

What is beyond time cannot be born and cannot die. It is uncreated and timeless.

Creation and everything in it is locked in time. What is born also dies and is not permanent.

The "why" of why the universe was born can never be known. Never.

The only thing to realize is that it does not really exist.

Day Eleven
APRIL 4, 1986

9:13 A.M. Slowly and ever so subtly a new and profound understanding of the nature of reality is making itself known to me. It is sublime and beautiful. The veil of illusion is slowly and gently being lifted. Through the darkness light is shining. Look too closely and it is gone...Let it be and it is always and ever present. Inwardly I bow to Poonjaji in gratitude for helping me to know my own true nature.

Yesterday morning while writing here I understood deeply that the Self is the only reality. It is the beginning and the end and all that is. It is beyond description and comparison. It is fullness and emptiness and that which perceives both. Finally it is beyond any kind of division or separation of any kind whatsoever.

It became obvious that only the Self can know the Self. All other than the Self is illusory and impermanent and therefore unreal.

During lunch with Poonjaji I burst out in uncontrollable laughter and joy at the ridiculous predicament that we are in. The absurdity of the truth that in fact the universe doesn't really exist. This made Poonjaji very happy.

In the evening Poonjaji said that he was pleased and that now he could "sleep well!"

He said that he no longer had any "relation" with me. He also said that now our real work could begin. That from now on our relationship (which he said no longer existed) would be beyond form and concept...

He said that we had a *real dialogue* and that this dialogue was not between two individuals but was in fact a dialogue of the Self. He was pleased. He said that this was very rare.

3:04 P.M. On arriving at Poonjaji's this morning I said to him that I understood that in time there would no longer be the need for any question and answer between us. That the teaching would be silent. He looked surprised and pleased when I said this. He then proceeded to tell me that he had prepared a "cooked" answer for me had I tried to ask him any questions today! He told me he would have replied strongly, saying there was no need. He said he had not yet shown me this side of his personality and I laughed and said now I had taken away his opportunity!

He said that now he and I were in "union." That it was unusual for this to happen so quickly. Also what has impressed him is that apparently I have received knowledge directly. That others experience bliss and other experiences and get lost in them — unable to proceed further. This pleased him a great deal. He was amazed that I told him the teaching would now be through silence. This was exactly his feeling and my saying it prior to his telling me proved the fact of our "union" being completed. He said now "things would happen."

Day Twelve
APRIL 5, 1986

Yesterday morning after the above agreement of our "union" Poonjaji went out with me and we went by rickshaw to change my traveller's checks at the State Bank of India. In the afternoon he took me to see the old Mogul palace and mosque of Lucknow. Majestic and beautiful. Magnificent!

Struck by Poonjaji's love. His gentleness and generosity. Giving in the most gentle and effortless manner. Never any sense that any effort whatsoever is being made in his generosity. Seems spontaneous and natural. More than unusual. Extraordinary. In fact, truly as a human being CAN be. Truly human. Nothing more actually, and this is the mystery. Too, too few human beings in this seemingly barbaric and inhuman world.

The same ease and lack of any kind of tension between us continues. Also last night, in spite of all that has occurred, I was watching my mind as boredom and doubt arose yet again. What a teaching! Just watch and learn...reminds me of "If ye had faith ye would not need miracles."

Another amazing letter arrived from one of Poonjaji's disciples yesterday. It was from the man who gave Poonjaji's address to Murray. He is from Australia and was here with his wife about three months ago. Yet another testimony to Poonjaji of Realization through his Grace. Totally convincing and full of clarity and profound gratitude. What more can I ask for? What more proof is required? From where does doubt arise in the face of truth? Doubt is, after all, one of the fetters — a most powerful foe — a dangerous enemy indeed.

Day Thirteen
April 6, 1986

This morning once again while sitting in the South Indian restaurant, I experienced a rush of clarity and understanding. Don't know if it's a result of meditation in my room prior to going there or due to this gentle unfolding of insight that I've found myself in the midst of since my contact with Poonjaji. Probably both—indeed as he has been telling me over and over they are one and the same—the "Self Nature" manifesting itself un-inhibited—flowing, touching—kissing me with insight.

After my arrival at Poonjaji's this morning and prior to our leaving for Dr. Singh's, he reiterated this point to make sure that it was clear to me. That our union began with the clear seeing of the fact that this "knowledge" or understanding had nothing to do with the individuals involved. It was *and only could be* once again: the SELF NATURE. Not he and not I. Only ONE SELF. That when this understanding is clear it sets the basis for a deep and profound meeting of two individuals—in the realization that they, as separate entities, do not have any separate existence. That they are both only manifesta-tions of one being—one source—that in the true seeing of this Fact, this Truth, there will be an absolutely Free and beautiful dance of the Self with the Self. A true union in emptiness. TRUE TEACHING which ultimately can only be the perception in silence of our—BEING.

This mysterious journey continues in spite of all the doubt and clinging of the mind to Samsara—the way things SEEM to be…

I understood today the need for absolute Non-abidance always and forever. Not to abide in any place is to not abide in this world. To not abide in the world means to BE in eternity—Freedom—Knowledge. Not to dwell upon or be captured by the mind and its endless preoccupations with itself and its past and present involvements with itself and its relation to the world. Simply not to dwell means there is space for the Self to manifest—to make itself known. Knowledge, wisdom, and insight will flow freely and naturally in a mind that does not dwell upon this world. Poonjaji mentioned this several times to me today.

Last night while reading different bits from Ramana's book, I saw how much I've been able to grasp finally about the relationship between the meaning of different types of samadhi and wisdom. For so long this has been troubling me and now, slowly, it's all becoming clear. No tension. Just clarity. No longer a problem. It's all perfect.

I bow down and touch Poonjaji's feet in gratitude for helping me to see my own Self. *Thank you. Thank you. Thank you.*

He is right—in fact he acts only as a *mirror* for others. Because he has no ego he can reflect our own Self nature back on ourselves. Therefore he remains free of involvement and responsibility as there is *no one acting or doing anything.* This is delightful in that this way we will develop and grow (or not) due only to our own inherent readiness and karma. Therefore he does nothing but serve as a catalyst to our own Self nature. He changes nothing, only helps what is already there. WHAT A

TEACHING! This is freedom in relationship, Indeed! (Talked with Poonjaji about this last night.)

On the morning of the 5th I said to Poonjaji that if we are in contact with the source of our being i.e. the Self, then we can reflect that light onto relative questions and effortlessly see and understand relative truths. This impressed him (and myself) as when I said it, it clearly was not coming from "me," but from the Source. Clarity and total confidence comes from clear perception and seeing from the Self. Contact = Being.

Only emptiness can perceive emptiness.

Yesterday afternoon Poonjaji told me several stories of people who had faith in him and had experienced miraculous and sudden cures from illnesses. I asked him if he used his will in these circumstances and he said no. That he had done so at one time but had always suffered for it. That he had "spontaneously" understood how to enter a person's mind, but in the exchange had always suffered, i.e. taking on their karma. Also, he felt that it was not ethical to do so. He said that he only acts as a mirror for others and that they will respond according to the purity of their disposition. In doing this he remains free of involvement and they get what they are suited for. Quietness, bliss, knowledge, Enlightenment, fear, etc. He very much liked my question about his use of will and said it was a subtle question although I honestly don't see why.

He told me last night that he saw a big change in me in the last two days. He asked me if I felt it and if I knew what it was. I answered not quite accurately in saying I had felt faith, trust, and a very subtle touching of the Self. He said it was the "Self Nature" manifesting—and that I looked and sounded totally different. The look in my eyes and the sound of my voice were radically changed. (I found it difficult to believe.) He told me to pay attention to what was happening now in the next few days—to relax and let things happen—to accept the "good with the bad" without reaction, seeing clearly and understanding that it all comes from the SELF. I mentioned that the final test was one of complete surrender (to the Self) and he agreed.

Feel much love for Poonjaji and feel much love coming from him...

Day Fourteen
April 7, 1986

Feel light, happy, quiet and free this morning...

Day Fifteen
April 8, 1986

I'm sitting on my bed and it's 12:45 A.M....So much has been happening! Where to begin?

This morning after waking, saw how *Freedom has no history.* Whatsoever. Freedom cannot exist with any solid entity known as past. It can only BE — FREEDOM IS ALONE. EMPTY and without attributes. DEATH MUST HAPPEN BEFORE FREEDOM CAN BE. The past must be let go of — must die. There is NO room for any history in the living timeless SELF.

Told Poonjaji that "Freedom has no history" on arrival this morning. He smiled, and said he had awakened this morning having a dialogue with me — very deep, he said. A point we hadn't touched upon yet, the end of all talk. He still felt it in his heart, but couldn't bring it back. He tried.

Feel so HAPPY! Felt a rush of bliss within me this afternoon. Joy and gentle bliss and so much love for Poonjaji! Is this all REAL? Told him that I felt blessed today and he was deeply touched, and tears came to his eyes. He said that this was the Self Nature talking and "what more could anyone say?" He was deeply moved by this and commented on it several times today. Went out with him to the river and then to the park. Felt a rush of bliss and joy and told him while walking back to his house that it is not to seek truth that is important but *TO BE truth* that was Enlightenment and perfect Freedom. He was moved again and said this was "fantastic."

Felt much love for him today — too, too much Love for him — I love him so! He said he was surprised that I was not acting "abnormally," meaning that I was not in tears or overwhelming emotion. That I was experiencing "equanimity" and this was better. He was pleased by this balance. Felt so much bliss and happiness being with him tonight.

Day Sixteen
APRIL 9, 1986

Told Poonjaji that *EMPTINESS REALLY MEANS LIMITLESS.* He was pleased when I said this. He said this understanding could only come from experience. We talked much about this. *Emptiness means no separation. No boundaries. Constant, beginningless, endless being!*

There is never any separation. *This is Enlightenment.* Enlightenment means no separation. Emptiness means limitless.

Full or empty mean the same thing. "Form is emptiness and emptiness is form." No separation *EVER.* Constant unbroken contact of NO-thing with ITSELF.

Earlier today we had talked about the "why" of existence i.e. the universe. The manifest universe is only the outward creative expression of the limitless uncreated Self.

The created is an expression of the uncreated — there is no difference ultimately between the two. They are one, and their nature is the same — empty.

Day Seventeen
April 10, 1986

11:02 P.M. I'm sitting on my bed in my room. David [a seeker visiting Poonjaji] came this morning....

I'm forcing myself to write now as I have *no* desire whatsoever to continue this journal. It is all happening by itself. The personality that wants to keep a record is losing the ability to keep up with what is happening... Today I felt waves of bliss welling up from within and with it, a deep feeling of a lack of interest in intellectual reflection and understanding i.e. of trying to grasp the ungraspable with a mind and intellect that simply cannot contain what is beyond itself. In spite of the fact that that is impossible, the INTEREST in doing so is dying. Replacing it is only a deep desire to abide in what IS, without any thought or reflection of any kind. I feel now that all this (thinking about it) is only a great impediment to the experience itself. I KNOW this to be so. I told Poonjaji this fact this morning and on hearing this his eyes lit up and then and several other times today he made clear to me in no uncertain terms that this was once again the SELF expressing itself. That the seeing and recognition of this clear understanding that thought and reflection are Death itself was fantastic and very, very important. (This is in fact the deep, deep willingness to finally really let go of the known....)

In silence is ALL. No Limitation. No Ego. Emptiness and Completeness, endless BEING and JOY.

This morning after we spoke, the bliss I had felt the day before yesterday started welling up inside me again. It continued until I came back to my room. Oddly enough, when I tried to meditate and was using "effort" to control my mind the flow stopped. I slept for forty-five minutes, and on waking, felt confused and unclear. I went back to Poonjaji's and we talked more about what happened in the morning. He is ten steps ahead of me always. He can always see clearly every time the Self Nature is manifesting—and often at these times it is so subtle that I am barely aware of its presence—and then without fail, he ALWAYS turns out to have been right. Then on going to the park to meet David I immediately felt the bliss welling up again. I had to force myself not to close my eyes (which I did eventually) so I could pay attention to the very interesting dialogue that Poonjaji and David were having. Then I sat in meditation for a long time. It's all happening by itself—effort is not involved—IT'S ALL TRUE!

Surrender and only Surrender is required.

Again tonight after dinner in his room I grew tired of the talk and only wanted to sit quietly. There was a lack of interest—more than that—a deep revulsion for the arising of thought and all that goes along with it.

I told Poonjaji yesterday that "I now have the courage and desire to die—but I don't know how." He said nothing at the time but brought it up today. He misses *nothing* that is important.

Now only to LET GO—let it happen.

On April 13th Andrew left Lucknow for two and a half weeks to visit friends in New Delhi and Bombay.

Day Twenty-one
APRIL 14, 1986
New Delhi

I'm sitting in Nirula's Restaurant. It's lunch time and it's crowded. Arrived in Delhi this morning.

The bliss continues in spite of all the doubt. I AM. Nothing to say. Empty. These words come from THAT.... Oh God—It's always there.

These last three days in Lucknow have been beyond words. On the morning of the 11th went to the zoo with Poonjaji and David. Afterwards talked with David outside and once again the bliss started welling up from within. Peace and Joy and Emptiness. Nothing at All! Who would believe it? Who *could* believe?

That afternoon again it started and I had to force myself to keep my eyes open. Oh! Oh! Oh! what can I say? It's here with me now. It's here and it's **nowhere!** Gentle, subtle, and abiding ALWAYS. I keep wondering if it will leave me and in spite of that it remains—to BE.

The evening of the 11th I grew tired of their talk and only wanted to BE QUIET.

On the 12th David GOT IT. Or so it seemed. I helped him to SEE. Then he and I had the most intimate being together two people can ever share. Also the SELF was coming through me so much that my hand was shaking. Then I left to buy my train ticket and held onto Nothing — after there was only Quietness within....

The next day David and I shared the silence together — it was beyond words and again — only nothing — sharing the silence — the silence which is empty and which reveals only simply what is...

Also going out with David in the evenings, having tea at Chaudhary restaurant it was there — coming through — and oh, the most fascinating sharing and discovering together of all this — it's too much, too wonderful!

Yesterday Poonjaji told me he had never had this kind of relationship with another person and how happy it made him and he cried. I was silent and felt only quietness and NOTHING else.

Then I think...is it still here? Has it left me? Has the emptiness gone forever?

The evening of the 12th it came again in my room. SILENCE.

In the talks with Poonjaji in these days — so, so, so much has been learned. Lifetimes of knowledge and truth and understanding — can all this be true?

Yesterday I proclaimed with tremendous conviction: "Anyone who tells you to do ANYTHING at all to attain Liberation is a liar and a cheater!"

Saying goodbye to Poonjaji I felt nothing at all. No emotion. I went to the park and sat on a bench before going to the station, and then there was only quietness and nothing else. Thought, yes, but it had no power. It was only chatter. The substratum was quietness and only being present.

Part Two

Diary and Letters
April – May 1986

"Murray, you should be the first one to read this letter since you brought him to me," Poonjaji said to me. It was a letter from Andrew, who had written from New Delhi. The following are extracts from that letter.

Dear Master

...I love you Master...The process has continued since I left you...You have entered me...I am dying Master, and soon there will be nothing left...There is only joy and love...I am somewhere beyond time and yet at the same time fully here...I feel the cells in my body are changing...Other people can feel it...You and I are One....

After I read Andrew's letter Poonjaji asked me, "What do you think this means?" "He is a Free man," I replied. Poonjaji nodded his head with great happiness. He said, "This man's conduct has been proper from the beginning."

Poonjaji said he was pleased that Andrew had left because he wanted to "test" him and find out what would happen while he was away.

Having left Poonjaji, Andrew underwent an explosive transformation, which he described in his diary:

At times the bliss that I would feel would seem almost unbearable. I thought that my body would not be able to stand the intensity of what I was feeling. Often at night, before sleeping, I felt it most strongly. I can only describe it as the actual physical experience of beginningless impersonal love — which is only the outward manifestation of the SELF — the Source and also the end of all that is — emptiness and fullness without limit, beyond concept, the living experience of beginningless endless BEING. It was even frightening at times as I realized that I was experiencing my own death. The Other was ALL and I saw that *this* was my own true SELF, and anything other than this was only illusory and had no inherent reality of its own. Only the SELF IS. This was *lived.*

Andrew immediately started having an impact on people he met. He spent six days with a young Israeli woman named Orly, whom he had met in India a few months earlier.

The bliss continued to come in waves, and now at times Orly also was having the same experience I was. I felt that my body could not withstand what was happening inside me. What had been happening to me continued on and off throughout each day, and her experience also grew in depth and intensity. At times we would share the fullness and bliss together. Indeed, at times we became one and there seemed to be no separation between us at all. Before my eyes I saw the illusion of her individuality fall away and it filled me with happiness.

The second week away from Poonjaji Andrew went to Bombay to visit Alka Arora, an Indian woman whom he had met in India two years earlier and would later marry.

Alka and I went to Elephanta Island together. The "Other" was there throughout the entire day. The feeling of absolute unity between the timeless and the relative felt more complete than ever before. I felt at once completely here and present, and at the same time totally away from and out of this world. In this there was total unity and integration. It was the Highest Bliss. There was no separation or division whatsoever. Absolute UNITY.

I sat with Alka on the beach watching the sunset. In the enveloping darkness we both were one and felt the bliss of Freedom without limit.

On leaving Bombay I felt no pain or anxiety in leaving Alka. The effortless detachment which had been with me since leaving Lucknow remained and I left feeling only the unbroken continuity of the present moment.

Andrew arrived back in Lucknow on April 29th. On May 2nd he wrote the following letter to Alka:

Dear Alka,

Where to begin? Each moment continues to be enough—one long PRESENT moment with no gap or break in continuity. I realized tonight that I've been back in Lucknow for three days now—but somehow the sense of the passing of time has faded out of my life. The eternal present always seems to be so engrossing that I rarely dwell on the past or worry about the future. I'm just fully where I am and am not grasping in any way— all without any effort or will. A strange kind of effortless detachment has become my permanent companion. Since I've returned to Lucknow much of the bliss and ecstasy has faded and what remains is a state of absolutely nothing special at all. NOTHING. Just life as it is. No attributes beyond an absolutely normal ordinary contact with the world as it is. It's like inwardly I've come full circle and finally once again I'm back where I started from: trees are in fact trees and mountains, mountains, etc. While talking with Poonjaji yesterday I grasped in a deeper way than I ever have before that there is no such thing as samsara. There is NO PROBLEM at all with or in this world. It is all absolutely perfect. All the conflict, suffering and confusion exist only in a mind that is in conflict. When we come to an end of conflict within ourselves, the outer conflict immediately ceases to be a problem. This does not mean that one ceases to have concern—but only that the *inherent reality* of the fact of conflict *ceases* to exist. There is NO conflict or confusion in this universe. Conflict and confusion arise only due to ignorance—but in fact—*ultimately the ignorance itself doesn't even exist!* It's all a great mystery Alka!

Today I was talking with Poonjaji about something he claims that he has not been able to discuss with anyone else—that is that this whole drama that we call life has *never ever* taken place—this very moment that I sit here writing to you has never actually occurred.... Intellectually this is impossible to grasp—even though I feel that this is true. This is the real Maya! This is the real mystery and this ungraspable fact can never truly be understood. It is beyond the human brain to grasp I think. My God—who would believe all this? My dear do I sound mad? I don't really understand it at all myself— although somewhere, somehow I feel that it *is* the way of things....

I have had a strange feeling these last two days. That is: what am I doing here? What is the point of this life? Deeply I saw that I no longer have any *interest* in life— human life as it is lived. It's so strange Alka! It's like— what am I doing here? What is it that I WANT from this life? And the answer comes = Nothing. Absolutely Nothing. In a strange way I feel (very subtly) like a stranger—an outsider in a world where I somehow no longer have any place. It's all quite bizarre, isn't it? It's strange in the fact that in spite of all I have said—I AM still here—fully human and VERY MUCH alive and present in this world. My dear I honestly don't fully grasp or understand anything that I have said. It's all coming from somewhere else. Somewhere deep, deep within that I am really not even conscious of. I say all that I have said—and it brings absolutely no feeling of fear or separation—and yet it all remains an *unknown*— a complete mystery to me—whoever me is that is writing this letter to you.

After I arrived an Indian disciple of Poonjaji's told me how Poonjaji had been speaking of me very often and was apparently very, very happy with what had happened to me. I told Poonjaji of what had taken place with you and Orly and he said that he had expected it and in fact had wanted me to leave in order to test what had taken place. He was not surprised at all and was very pleased. The night I arrived, as I was about to leave, we embraced and he kissed me and I him, and he said something like, "This is a love affair." In spite of this I continue to feel no emotion at all. The next day I told him this as I had been thinking about how odd it was. I said, "I feel no connection with you and at the same time no separation at all." I explained that this was indeed different from a feeling of "communion"—as communion is still a feeling—something, and in fact I felt nothing at all. No connection and no separation. This is a different thing almost impossible to describe. When I said this tears came to his eyes. He said, "Who could understand this?" He told me that he had intended to tell me soon that there was something higher which I had not grasped yet—but I had told him this, and this was what he had wanted to explain to me. He said that he had intended to wait to tell me this as he thought I wouldn't be ready to understand it yet.

The night I arrived I had a dream about Dr. Singh. I remember nothing except that I saw Dr. Singh facing me and his body and face were luminous—shining, and in this, blurred. When I arrived at Poonjaji's the following morning I told Poonjaji that I had a dream about Dr. Singh. In the afternoon (the 30th) Dr. Singh and his wife came for their usual biweekly visit. I was sitting next to Dr. Singh and I was talking with Poonjaji about the known and unknown. Suddenly Dr. Singh jumped up and ran to Poonjaji and grabbed him in an embrace — again and again he embraced him and bowed his head to touch Poonjaji's lap. Poonjaji exclaimed, "THE EGO IS BROKEN!" Dr. Singh sat down next to me and was silent and could not speak. Poonjaji looked at him for a long time with tears in his eyes and we all sat in silence. Poonjaji later explained that only by hearing Poonjaji and I talk — in one instant of recognition through listening, Dr. Singh was Enlightened — ??!!

My God Alka who would believe all this? What's even more far out is this: In the evening after this had happened I was sitting in Poonjaji's room and we were talking. Then suddenly I remembered the dream that I had had the night before — and Poonjaji said that in this dream — "Dr. Singh's 'work' had been done for him." I asked him more about it — feeling there must be a connection but not being able to really believe it or understand it. Poonjaji told me I didn't have to believe it or understand it — but that it was true — !

Alka I don't understand any of this myself — I'm only telling you what has taken place....

Today Poonjaji told me that our work was finished. That we would continue to be friends but that our formal relationship was over. He then said that he wanted me to "accept responsibility for the work." I just listened silently and felt no reaction one way or the other. In fact I felt nothing at all — neither for or against what he said. I just accepted it and said nothing. What this means I don't even know — but I have no desire to "do" any work — nor do I have any aversion to it either. Strange isn't it? I also don't even know what it means and I also feel totally unconcerned or worried about it. What will be, will be, and this will have nothing to do with my desire or will. He then told me again that he has had to make no effort in trying to help me and that this has never happened before with anyone else. I asked him why this was so and he said something like the preparation or readiness was there when I came to see him.

Well, I guess that's about all. Poonjaji has had much trouble deciding where he wants to go and also feels weak and not confident of his stamina. I will contact Orly in Delhi on the 4th. Please tell me what has been happening inwardly since we parted. I'll call you from Delhi when I get there.

With much affection and Love,

Andrew

On May 3rd, Andrew wrote the following letter to his mother and older brother in New York:

Dear Luna and Joshua,

I am writing this letter to both of you. Josh, I am sorry that I forgot your birthday. I was so absorbed in my own life that I completely forgot about your birthday and I apologize. I send a big Hug and much, much Love to you. This letter is the letter that I promised to write to you when we spoke on the phone; also it is an answer to Luna's last two letters.

This is a difficult letter for me to write. I have been wanting to write it for the last two or three days, but have felt that quite frankly, I didn't know how to write it, how to explain all that has happened to me over the last five weeks. I would prefer if both of you would keep all I have to say to yourselves, for nobody will understand it.

Something very radical has happened to me. Something very big, and at the same time, nothing special at all. Quite simply, a part of me has died and with that death, in a sense I have been reborn. My past has ceased to have any influence on my being. I have become, in a very mysterious way, free of the bondage of my past, and of time. The pain, the misery, the endless dwelling on the tragedy of my personal history is over. There is no more identification with Andrew's past. It has become a memory only and it no longer is a source of concern. The need to understand it, to overcome it, is gone. In fact it is finished. And when it is finished it seems as if it never even happened. When we finish with our past, *really finish with it,* in an instant, a sense of unparalleled freedom makes itself known. In this freedom, where there is no influence from the past, is where we discover our true nature, the source of our being. There is nothing special or extraordinary in this, as this is who we already are, always have been, and always will be. Beyond the illusion of personality and time, our true nature always is. We already are free, but the problem is that we don't realize it and due to conditioning, believe that we are who we think we are: separate individuals, with separate personal histories, isolated and alone in this big and often frightening world. When we come to the point where we are *finally* ready to let go of this idea of separateness, which means letting go of everything we have ever known, then we see clearly that there is nothing to fear. There is nothing inherently wrong or evil in this world we are living in. It is only due to ignorance that we have fear, and it is this *fear alone* that is the source of all evil. How or when this ignorance began I don't know and I don't know if anyone really does. In fact it's not really important, for the only important thing is to discover and realize within ourselves that the ignorance is not real and never has been real. It doesn't exist at all and the only reality is our own true "Self-nature"; which is freedom itself and is manifested in this world in the form of boundless, beginningless, impersonal Love and Joy.

When I came to Lucknow to meet Poonjaji five weeks ago, I came here with no expectations and even a fear. I had come to meet another teacher and felt absolutely that I didn't want to get involved yet again with another teacher, another personality and ultimately more bondage and disappointment. I wanted to be free of all that. So why did I come? I was drawn here and felt I had to come, even though I felt much resistance and fear about what I might be getting myself into yet again. Something "clicked" on my very first meeting with Poonjaji. We were talking about the need to make "effort" in practice and Poonjaji said to me that in fact this itself was the problem, that it was in making absolutely no effort at all that freedom could be known. When he told me this, for some reason it penetrated very deeply and I had a sudden understanding that he was right. I "saw" it and the seeing only lasted two seconds—but it had a deep impact and our relationship began in that moment. I spent almost three weeks with him after that, usually eight hours a day, often talking a great deal and also many times just sitting in silence. Much was gone into and much understood. All the nagging questions that I have had over the last four years about different forms of spiritual experience and the results of different forms of meditation practice were all gone into in depth. All the questions I have had that nobody could help me with, and which had troubled me greatly were all answered. When I told him in detail about the spontaneous awakening that I had when I was sixteen, he told me that at that moment I had experienced all there was to experience, and he said that if I had had a teacher or someone whom I could have talked to about it, a man of knowledge—then my work would have been over then. Much of what I understood then has returned, and with that and much more I have been able to grasp and understand so, so much. I can hardly believe it all myself. After about a week or so with this man, finding our talks so, so satisfying, I unconsciously and consciously surrendered to him—*realizing that he was only my own Self* and since then I have been a free being. There is so much to say and explain! I can't possibly say it all in a letter. With each passing day he expressed more and more pleasure at how my understanding was progressing. He many, many times was praising me and exclaiming things that he saw were happening which I *never* believed when he said them. I always felt that he was completely exaggerating the truth and it made me feel uncomfortable and caused me to doubt him. But—I discovered with time that each and everything that he saw became a living experience for me, and it only took me time to catch up with him as ultimately all turned out to be my experience. It is just that he can see truth directly and due to my being hypnotized by a lifetime of a very gross state of awareness—the perception of the *subtle nature* of the living reality took time for me to see. I have never ever in my life experienced such appreciation from another human being. It's all more than I can grasp! And to be honest I don't identify with any of it either. It's all part of the magic as none of what has been understood here has been understood by Andrew. The ego simply cannot grasp what is beyond itself. The SELF can only know the SELF and in this understanding there is no personality or ego involved. There cannot be if the understanding is real. Can you both follow all this? It's really too marvelous and too wonderful to be believed! When I left Lucknow two and a half weeks ago he told me with tears in his eyes that he had never had this same intimacy with anyone else—and many people have been Enlightened through contact with him. Again I just listened passively and somehow this didn't lodge in my ego—I just listened and let it go. Nothing, Nothing—I FELT NOTHING. I know this is hard to believe but it's *true.* This *is* true because the core of our relationship doesn't take place between two personalities. It is only the SELF knowing the SELF. That's why Andrew felt nothing—for he is *not involved.* What I am about to tell you both now is some-

40

thing that I hesitate to tell. I hesitate because it is in fact too much to be believed. I don't even believe it myself but I know it's true because it happened.

Poonjaji had told me at one point that he and I had become one. I said, "You mean Communion," and he told me, "No, Communion is between two—we are in Union—that means One and not TWO." Again I didn't believe him or even understand what he was saying. I left Lucknow two and a half weeks ago and I discovered after saying goodbye to him that I felt no emotion whatsoever. *None.* This has continued throughout my trip to Delhi and Bombay and up until my return to Lucknow five days ago. I understood ultimately that he was right— how can you miss your own Self? I left Lucknow for Delhi and met my friend Orly there. I spent six days with her and then I went to Bombay where I spent seven days and saw Alka. Soon after my arrival in Delhi the impact of what had taken place in Lucknow began to make itself known. I spontaneously began to experience waves of bliss and love that at times were so strong that I felt my body wouldn't be able to contain it. But in this Bliss there was no loss of clarity or understanding. In fact this only *deepened* much of what I already understood and in a way I cannot describe in words—the understanding of what it means to *die to the known* was lived. It was at times even a little frightening, as I knew and saw that a part of me was dying and that I had somewhere stepped out of this world into the Unknown. I consciously and unconsciously surrendered—making even a conscious decision to finally let go and give up my life—Andrew's life, for Absolute Freedom — which really means to let go of EVERYTHING. Then the most startling and surprising thing of all happened: People whom I spent time with could feel what had happened to me and were even affected by my presence. I spent five or six days with Orly — spending hours talking about what had happened in Lucknow and before my eyes — she began to experience the same bliss and understanding that I was! I couldn't believe it, and also somehow it all seemed perfectly natural. Simply by the fact that she loves me very much and TRUSTS me implicitly — the Self nature in her was able to recognize itself by opening up to me. It works like a mirror. One's own SELF is reflected and seen when one has faith in another who can be as a clear reflector. When the EGO has been cracked (so to speak) the light of the Self shines through unobstructed. If one has implicit faith and *trust* in someone who sees clearly then — if many factors come together (some of which are unknown) then the light of one's own Self makes itself known. This has nothing to do with effort or will but has only to do with an *inner readiness* to SEE and an inner surrender and trust. The rest happens by itself and effort only serves to obstruct the light. The same thing happened with Alka — my God I couldn't believe what was taking place before me! Who would believe it? Who could believe it?

I arrived back in Lucknow five days ago. Since my return much of the bliss has faded and I have returned to an absolutely normal state of consciousness. Nothing but *life as it is.* The only thing is that there is an unbroken sense of continuity and evenness throughout each day. Nothing special. But there is a sense of being always in the present with much contentment and calm. I feel little or no desire for other than what IS and the present moment always feels like enough. There is no fear and no longing. I also realized yesterday that from now on inwardly I would always be alone. A strange feeling but without any sense of sadness in any way. I told Poonjaji about this and he told me that in fact I had only come home to the actual truth of human existence. Then I realized he was right. I myself had said many times in the past that the truth was we are born alone and we die alone.

Poonjaji told me two days ago that "our work was over." That we would continue to be friends but our **work** was done. He then said that he wanted me to "accept responsibility for the work." When he said this I just listened passively and accepted what he said without judgement. I have no desire to "do" any "work" and I have no aversion to it either. What will be will be and it won't be up to me anymore but to other forces that are Unknown and to which I have surrendered. (I haven't flipped—this unknown I refer to is Truth—or the SELF.)

I'm sure that both of you have been quite startled and amazed by what I have explained. *I am too!* If I wake up tomorrow morning and I find all I have told you is no longer true—then I will not have lied or said an untruth in any way. I have been a witness to all this in the same way that you have been a witness in reading this letter.

There is more and wild (hard to believe) things that I have left out due to that it is not important and would take too much time to explain — and also much of it can't be explained as it is all beyond the rational mind to grasp — the human mind for that matter!

I told Poonjaji this afternoon that I intended to write a letter to my mother and brother telling about the last five weeks but I told him that I didn't know how as it was all too much to be believed. He replied that "This kind of letter will make an effect!"

It's now 4:45 A.M. I can hear the birds singing outside welcoming in the new morning. I have stayed up all night writing this to you both....

Poonjaji will come to Delhi on the 11th and after a few days there I will go up to Haridwar with him. Murray will meet us there and I think others will also come. All this could change but that's how things stand as of today.

I love you both VERY much.

Andrew

What follows are the last entries of Andrew's diary:

MAY 5, 1986   11:16 P.M.
Coffee shop at Clark Hotel
Lucknow

Don't be good. Let goodness BE.

I feel drunk. Drunk with Joy. For absolutely
NO REASON AT ALL. HA HA HA HA HA!!!!

So much to write and why do I feel there is
NOTHING TO SAY?

I I I I I I I
I I I I I I I

Don't even Know!

Why say anything? Who COULD keep a record of all
this other-worldly magic and mystery? What does it ALL
MEAN ANYWAY?

ONLY

FREEDOM   ! ! !

HA!

MAY 6, 1986
Sitting at Clark's — yet again.

So here I am attempting to begin again in this journal of evolution, of rebirth and rediscovery of The Reality. Freedom itself and absolutely NOTHING AT ALL. So, so, so, so much every single day! Every moment is yet another moment of learning and self-discovery. How can I keep a record of something that never ceases to BE? My mind is or has been BLOWN completely out of this world. It is in shreds! Nothing solid left. Nothing to hold onto and no concepts left. Only open space and absolutely nowhere to stand. NOWHERE AT ALL.

This morning I showed Poonjaji what I wrote spontaneously here last night on the preceding page. He said: "Now there is no inner and no outer."

This afternoon in the park several of Poonjaji's Indian devotees asked me questions about my "Enlightenment." (Poonjaji has apparently been praising me very highly and telling them that I am Enlightened.)

Without hesitation or self-consciousness I was able to answer all their questions to their satisfaction. I didn't identify with what I said at all. Also I felt much love and warmth for them and felt the same coming from them. Then one of them, a kind old man, thanked me, showing such love, praise and appreciation that I couldn't understand why he was saying all that to me. If I don't live another day in this world his love will be the most blessed love I have ever felt from another human being in my life! I shall never forget it. And also, yet again, NONE of this lodged in my ego. I don't know why but I know that it did not. I just listened, felt very touched, but took none of it personally—just listened and let it go—again *all without any effort at all.*

On and on and on and NOTHINGNESS IS ALL.

I have heard more miracle stories from Poonjaji's life in these last three days than could ever, ever be believed or accepted by most people. I know every one of them is true and they also neither trouble me nor inspire me. They just ARE and it's just more of what IS.

Nothing and everything are one and the same.

Having no belief is absolute freedom to KNOW.

NO DREAMS / NO CONCEPTS / NO HOPES
IS IS IS OPENNESS
TO ALL THAT HAS NO LIMIT.

Absolute Discrimination is Absolute Freedom.
NO BONDAGE IS NO BOUNDARIES.

LOVE IS THE ONLY REALITY.

This did not come out of reflection or thought—it CAME FREELY FROM NO-WHERE.

My Master is my SELF. / Poonjaji. LOVE.

Who am I?

MAY 7, 1986   10:40 P.M.
Clark Hotel

This I feel must be the end of all that has come before in this record of one man's journey home. It will be the end of that, and then there will be the beginning of the outcome of all that has occurred at the feet of my Master. What will take place from this moment on will no longer be from my own will or desire but will only flow from Him. Andrew's life, in a sense, has now come to an end. His will is my will and his desire my own. I am he and there is total freedom in this. Andrew has no investment or involvement in this in any way. Somewhere Andrew no longer is. He is no longer in control — or desires to be in control. He has surrendered totally and completely to his Master — which is ultimately only his own true SELF. No plans — no personal needs, or painfully unfulfilled desires. He is empty now and is free to be of help — Again — there is no identification with any of this. He has no feeling for or against — there is only surrender and faith. The rest will only be...(Could anyone reading this understand that none of this is me?)

This is a record of what took place today in Lucknow:

I woke up at 7:30 A.M., took a bath, and went to the train station and tried to buy tickets for Poonjaji and myself to go to Delhi on the ninth or tenth. None were available and I went to his house at 9:00 A.M. I ate breakfast there and then went up to his room. He had obviously been resting when I arrived and I had there-

49

fore not wanted to disturb him. He told me he had been dreaming about me. He had been in a dialogue with me. Exclaiming "Have it!" to me forcefully while simultaneously lifting his arm, he had woken up. We talked. He told me again as he had the day before that he could feel that his body was slowly dying. That the elements which had been borrowed for the vehicle to live now had been used and wanted to return from where they came. That his "loan" was now over. With tears in his eyes he smiled at me and said, "Now I can go." The smile and what he said had meant that now that we had met—he felt he could leave this world. I just looked at the ground. We went downstairs and I showed him what I had written here last night. When he read, "My Master is my SELF / Poonjaji—Love —" he cried and said, "See what I mean?" Again referring to the fact of our union. He also talked about waking up and saying to me, "Have it." He was very moved and—said again "See what it means?" or something like that. I bowed to him and was quiet. He talked more about it but I can't remember what was said.

This morning Poonjaji said to me as he had yesterday that I had the same look in my eyes as Ramana did. He said that he'd seen these eyes only three times in his life: in Ramana's, his own, and mine. I listened, and not really believing it, said that I couldn't see this. He said to see this one had to look into one's own eyes objectively, as if looking at another. Only then would it be possible to see this.

After lunch I went to a restaurant and had chai [Indian tea] and read my book. As I had felt totally exhausted all morning, I went back to my room, took a bath, and slept. Immediately upon lying down I had a dream: It was evening and Poonjaji was on a bicycle going down a road away from me and he told me to go in another direction toward which he pointed his arm. He said something like "go that way" or "go there" and proceeded on his way down the road. I woke up and discovered that the dream had only lasted a few minutes as I had looked at my watch and it was 3:30. I had just lain down. I immediately went back to sleep and slept until 5:00 which I had intended to do.

At 5:00 P.M. I got up, had a chai, and went to the park to meet Poonjaji. At the entrance to the park I met the Singhs who were also on their way to meet him. We embraced and then saw Poonjaji and Mr. Sharat coming from the other entrance to the park. Meeting Poonjaji I exclaimed, "I had a dream about you. You were on a bicycle going down a road telling me to go the other way." His face lit up with surprise and joy and he said, "I had the same dream." We talked about it and discovered that indeed he had had the dream at precisely the same time I had: 3:30 P.M. He was as genuinely surprised at this as I was. He then told me he had decided I should proceed on to Rishikesh on my own and that he would go to Delhi with his family on the fifteenth. I went back to the station and tried for a long time to get a ticket in first class and then in second class and also talked to the ticket supervisor about the tourist quota. He told me I could get tourist quota only from an office in Hazrat Ganj. I went to Poonjaji's from there and arrived at 7:40 P.M.

When I arrived he was reading a copy of The Mountain Path that had arrived in the morning. He read an article about Krishnamurti aloud to Mr. Sharat and myself. He then exclaimed about how marvelous this fact of our having the same dream had been. We went down for dinner at 8:30 and returned to his room about 9:00 P.M.

We talked more about the dream. I asked him, "Whose dream was it?" He went into this a little and then said the dream was only a confirmation of what had already been happening. He said, as he had already told me, "Our work together is over." He said that my understanding of his teaching was total and he wanted me to go out and help others. The dream of the bicycle was saying this. Also his dream upon waking, telling me to "have it." He said that he was very pleased with me. That although others had also been liberated through contact with him, I possessed the ability to express clearly this teaching in a way that no other person had yet been able to. He said, "You leave people nowhere to stand." He said I would be able to express this teaching clearly to others and would be of help to people. He said I shouldn't be selfish—responding to the fact that I obviously wanted to be with him longer. He said he now felt "free" and at peace and that he no longer felt the burden of carrying on the teaching. I could do it now, and for this he was relieved and felt free to die. He no longer had the will or desire to continue living. Then he told me that the kind old gentleman devotee of his had spoken to him about me in the park this afternoon. The devotee had said that he had been thinking of me all night and about what I had said to him the day before. He also told Poonjaji that somehow he had felt it was Poonjaji who had prompted him to ask me the questions that he did. I said, "Why? What did I say? Why? This is not me he is talking about."

When I got up to leave I embraced Poonjaji and he slapped me on the back and said, "Have it!"

Andrew wrote to his mother from Lucknow on May 13th.

…The love affair between Poonjaji and me continues. The dialogue continues and so does the amazing experience of KNOWING again and again—that things are indeed **not at all** as they seem to be….If all unfolds as Poonjaji feels sure it will, then all will be known at the right time. I have stepped into the unknown and from now on—all is—unknown to me.

Part Three

Letters
May – July 1986

Andrew arrived in Rishikesh on May 16th. We met by the Ganges River just outside of Rishikesh and he told me everything that Poonjaji had said. He had no plans except to wait with Orly and me for Poonjaji to arrive.

The impact of Orly's meeting with Andrew was continuing to have a profound effect on her. After two days Alka arrived from Bombay, and she too remained deeply affected. As a direct result of one talk with Andrew, I was also undergoing a transformation.

On May 19th, Andrew wrote the following letter to Poonjaji:

Dear Master,

I am here with Murray and several others. Much "work" is going on and Meditation is constant throughout the entire day. Two women are in ecstasy and Murray has opened up to me and the "Process" has started within him. I have no more doubts about anything. I accept fully the responsibility and my life is yours MASTER: Your will is mine and my Love YOUR OWN. Please come soon.

    In silence

Andrew

We would sit together for hours at tea shops and spend long periods of time in silence. All was transcended through Andrew's presence and words.

After ten days in Rishikesh, Andrew and I went to visit Poonjaji in New Delhi. When we arrived, Andrew asked Poonjaji excitedly if he knew what was happening in Rishikesh and he replied, "Yes, and more. This is an appointment with the Absolute. Some people are here to teach meditation and some to speak about the Truth, but once in a rare time for the good of mankind someone comes along who can Enlighten others, and you are such a one."

The effect of this meeting on Andrew was not noticeable until we left New Delhi. It started showing itself on the train back to Rishikesh the following morning. Immediately upon opening his eyes Andrew looked at me and said, "I am always like you are in deep sleep." Later that morning when I told Andrew what he had said, he was surprised. He told me he had no recollection of his words.

The impact of Andrew's meeting with Poonjaji continued to reveal itself. The first evening of his return to Rishikesh we gathered around Andrew and began to ask him questions. This overwhelmed him and he found it difficult to respond. A powerful presence filled the room. Andrew seemed lost, and appeared to be at the mercy of something much greater than himself. He said, "I feel helpless."

The next day Andrew went to the post office and received the following letter from Poonjaji dated May 20th:

Dear Beloved ONE,

I am not running away from schedule. I had in view to stay on in Delhi for seven days to leave you **ALONE, FREE** and **INDEPENDENT.** You have to take up the entire responsibility to help the true seekers with no teaching or any kind of foothold for the mind to abide. The patch of cloud imagined to have covered the sun has to vanish by itself. Would you help Murray. He needs Love apart from anything else. I like him but he never opened to me. If I told him you need no effort just **BE.** He said, "You Rascal!!! I have to make strong effort, the Maharshi said so." Good luck but who won wisdom with effort? The Maharshi told me, "Keep QUIET." I will write to you to come to Delhi to accompany me to Haridwar in a couple of days....

Love — Love — Love

H. W. L. Poonja

Andrew phoned his mother in New York on May 31st. "Come over, there's something wonderful happening here, you won't believe it. Don't ask questions. I'll tell you when you get here. Just come over."

Andrew received a letter from Poonjaji dated June 2, 1986:

My own Self

in the form of an American,

Love, much Love,

Did you receive my letters? Some have come back to me because they were no longer needed! (I enclose one of them.)

I am returning to my normal physical shape quickly. I need more care at Delhi so that I can give you good company while walking and swimming.

What has happened around you. I am so Happy.

H. W. L. Poonja

On June 10th Andrew received another letter in reply to one of his:

O Virtuous Man!
Excellent — Excellent.

I am very happy to read the said anonymous letter [from you] rising from the Unknown, Beyond, Self Nature. The suffering human race needs you to help them to live a Happy Life of Love and friendship. Yes, we will stay again together at Rishikesh when your mother arrives in India....

I wish to see Alka Arora and Orly before they leave India at Rishikesh, Haridwar or Delhi....

Love, dear one, Your own Self

H. W. L. Poonja

We lived in great joy as one family and Andrew was growing to trust himself more and more as a teacher. The tea shop by the river became a place of intense discussion. We slept few hours. One day the lady who brought us milk came and asked, "Who are you people, what are you doing? You are showing so much love."

On June 24th Andrew met his mother in New Delhi. She was shocked at seeing the changes in her son. His confidence and authority astonished her. On meeting her in Delhi Poonjaji boldly declared, "He's my son! My son!"

Meanwhile, my visa was coming to an end and I would be going to England on July 2nd. Prior to my leaving India, I spent two days with Poonjaji in New Delhi. On July 2nd I wrote the following letter to Andrew:

Dearest Andrew and friends,

I saw Poonjaji yesterday — his eyes like two coals — he has not come for two reasons. 1) His foot swelling 2) to give [you] more time...

I asked him if he thought things would go so fast — he said yes and that the momentum will continue and there will be "a revolution among the young — so far no one has been able to do it." He said you deserve it and we both agreed you are flawless…I felt like bowing to everyone I saw last night — the light from Poonjaji's eyes was identical to the light in me. He definitely wants to spend time with you.

Karl [a western student] asked me, "Did Poonjaji confirm what's happening?" I said, "There is no need, he knows who Andrew is."

Much love and thanks,

Murray

I asked Andrew if he would come to England, as I knew many people there who would be interested in his teachings. He accepted my invitation and I returned to England to make the necessary arrangements.

Part Four

Letters between
Andrew and H.W.L. Poonja

September 1986 – March 1989

September 17, 1986
Haridwar

My own Self
I have your letter dated 8th Sept. from Bangkok.
Excellent! Excellent. Gone beyond.
Wonderful description of the undescribable nonentity!
I am back home. The Swami is here too and other Indians.

I have found a man who would transmit Light to the suffering world.

    Love you, Alka, Murray.

Will you write to me more and more about what never Happened?

    O my love
    I hug you, kiss you and what not.
    Your own Self
        H. W. L. Poonja

October 6, 1986
Totnes, England

Dear Master,

Oh Master! So much power! *Your wish is being fulfilled!* I have been in England ten days now. I'm staying with Murray and Shanti. I have seen about ten people already and Master I am on *FIRE!* The teaching is coming through me in new ways all the time and the higher power is expressing itself creatively. The TRUTH is EVERNEW and SHINES BRIGHTLY MASTER through your own true SON & SELF. MASTER I LOVE YOU I LOVE YOU I LOVE YOU I LOVE YOU. You are in me and your power is helping others. Your desire Master is mine for I have no choice for surrender is all I know. *What is it* Master? *What is it* that is doing all this? I have been seeing people everyday all day without a break and I find that the more work I do the stronger your power flows through me. I often feel carried away these days Master, drunk on the wine that is YOU and talking like a man drunk. My only wish is to intoxicate those around me forever — forever to be FREE and Happy Master — wanting only that they let the divine power manifest in them and be their own true SELF. This SELF KNOWLEDGE — to impart this — is my only mission. To make them aware only of their own true *Natural State* before creation even was a thought. The teaching Master is Only Love and the teacher is only Love. LOVE LOVE AND ONLY *THAT* in which there is NOTHING, Master, absolutely *NOTHING* AT ALL! Master I am *DRUNK!*

You see Master my intention was to write to you and tell you all the details of my time here but my pen was also drunk and I write like a man gone Mad!

We have been looking for a house and I hope to have one within one week. Alka and the others that were with me in India will come and stay with me. Already I have two letters from people in Holland who want to come and also a woman from Canada whom my mother spoke to will fly over to see me in a month. The news here in Totnes is traveling fast — Much, Much work to do. Murray has done much to prepare the way. He is doing well.

I have decided not to go to my brother's wedding in Taiwan in December. The needs of many people are far more important than going to one man's wedding. When I get the house here I will have open Satsang every evening and see people individually during the day. I will plan to come back to India to see you when my work is done here — probably in about three months. PLEASE WRITE OFTEN.

IN LOVE, YOUR SON & SELF

Andrew

October 19, 1986
Totnes, England

Dear Master,

I wrote a letter to you ten days ago. I hope that you have received it. Oh Master! Who could believe all this? Almost every day I have been seeing people privately during the day and every evening a group of people gather at Murray's house for Satsang with me in the evenings. So much so fast! I am amazed and at the same time, no matter what, I never feel that any of this has anything at all to do with me. It's like watching a fascinating movie. I remain always firmly rooted in my seat, never moving and somehow always distant and removed, while at the same time totally and fully present and *AWARE*. The power of the unknown for about four days in a row was indeed overwhelming this small mortal body. A few days ago I felt as if this body had become in some way like a generator—able to generate huge amounts of energy in response to the needs of those who come to me. The power of it is so strong at times that I felt if one were not somehow prepared for this, the nervous system would simply burn up due to overload. Oh Master! My Love for You is my life and it is *ONLY UNCONDITIONAL SURRENDER* that has made any of this possible. Surrender and only Surrender is the beginning, the middle and the end of this path and it is only this that I know. I love you Master. My relationship with you is the only relationship that I have. For ALL the others, it is only Your Love, THAT UNKNOWN, that is flowing from me to anyone who truly wants to

BE FREE. Several people here are doing very well and one woman was Enlightened in her first talk with me! We have found a fantastic three bedroom house and are going to move into it on Oct. 24th. My mother also will come soon for six weeks. A woman who heard about me through my mother will fly here to see me next month. Three people from Holland are coming also. Next week a meditation teacher from London is coming for four days. It's strange Master but I get the feeling that some of the meditation teachers here are intimidated by me — why?? What has anybody got to lose? The power of the Silence during Satsang is overwhelming at times — and I invite anyone to ask any questions at all that they like....

Things are moving so fast here — It's unbelievable. We are taking the house for three months beginning Oct. 24th. Full pranam *and all my Heart.*

YOUR SON & OWN SELF

Andrew

October 30, 1986
New Delhi

My own Self,

We returned from Haridwar. I have read your letters dated 6th and 19th Oct. '86 along with others....I have replied to all the letters only your letters remained to be replied but I took out twenty photostat copies of your letters and have sent them to people who could understand that which is beyond understanding, and have been working with me to comment on the above letters.

I am very happy upon YOU. You are a Virtuous man, you stood on the mountain of merits to peep unto the Supreme Secrets of unknown, unheard of, Beauty, that remained untouched, unseen hitherto, has offered ITSELF to hug you and swallow the phenomenal mystery to reveal itself to ITSELF. O Andrew, my dear you have done it, every BE-ing will have Peace and Love and Light in your Presence.

Did you keep the copy of the letters, if not may I send you the xerox copies of your letters dated 6th and 19th Oct. Please tell Alka or Orly or Orit to record every word that dropped from your lips spontaneously.

H. W. L. Poonja

November 14, 1986
Totnes, England

Dear Master,

I received your letter written on October 30th and I am humbled Master, deeply humbled. I have no words to express the wonder that is my permanent companion each and every day as I witness this explosion that is taking place around me. Oh Master! Who could believe all this is taking place? The power of what is going on here is too much for the rational mind to accept — and yet, myself and those near to me have no choice but to accept that which is beyond comprehension. Each evening after Satsanga is over and the people leave we sit around together in mutual awe of that which is occurring here. Master I know that you knew all this would take place — and so once again and forever Master *I am only YOURS. My only relationship is with YOU* — YOU and only YOU and in this relationship there is NONE for I am YOU and in this together we are NOT. There is NOTHING that separates us for you have absorbed me completely into YOUR*SELF*. In THAT I am no more. There is only you and in YOU there is NO me and NO YOU but only NOTHING, EVERYTHING and in that Master Only the MYSTERY that is ALWAYS UNKNOWN. That alone is your true face and yet I can never see You clearly for how can the Self see the Self? It is impossible — the Self can only KNOW itself, that is ALL.

I abide in YOUR HEART and that is my own SELF. From this HOME I never move but abide in the stillness that was forever untouched by the illusion of form and change.

Forever I am your child and my innocence is my only security for that security lies only in NOT KNOWING.

Three evenings ago I said to the group, "My home is the Heart and my refuge is NOT KNOWING."

Master — what can I say to YOU? YOU who KNOWS ALL and is forever silent? What can I say for you know more about this mystery than I. Each day it unfolds yet again and I become quiet as I realize the immeasurable and unknowable silence that screams so loudly — it declares only It-SELF, and in THAT, all is destroyed.

My Love to You forever

My Love to You forever

My Love to You forever

MY LOVE is — YOU

I am busy all the time seeing people and six nights a week we have Satsanga here in the evenings. More people are coming all the time and a lady arrived two days ago from Holland to spend time with me. We are living together here in a beautiful house in the country and our being together in this way is a living example of how human beings can live together in Love and Harmony. Murray has just moved in with us for one week. Several others also want to come and stay here for a few days or a week but there simply isn't room for all that. They come here often but want to be able to immerse themselves more in the Love and bliss that we are all sharing together.

I will stay here till I am invited to go somewhere else. Whatever happens though I would like to come and spend a few weeks with you at the end of January or early February.

Please write to me!

Everyone sends their Love to You, especially Murray!

Your own TRUE SON & SELF

Andrew

November 11, 1986
New Delhi

My own dear SELF,

I hug you and kiss your HEART! And Love my own Self like Narcissus. I have read your letters and have taken photostat copies and have dispatched to those who are really deserving to read something Beyond language and have read their reactions who give you a status of ancient Seers — Rishis of the Vedas or the Buddha reincarnated to once again help the suffering humanity!

Write to me more and more about what happens before you. I want to speak unto you something which has never been said, why, Because I and You never exist, therefore we could speak between us. You have occupied my whole mind day and night, I do not know what Romance is being enacted by both Lovers to each other.

With Love to you and all other members of my own Family.

Love

H. W. L. Poonja

November 17, 1986
New Delhi

Dear Andrew

I am leaving India for U.S.A. early Jan. '87. You have not so far sent any copy of your students' letters. I want to know how they all understand you, or simply they waste your time. Your time is much more precious and need not be wasted to speak to the unworthy egoistic people of this planet. I have to uncover more sacred secrets to you, when and where I can't say. I told you, you go and teach we will meet later. If my visit to the U.S.A. materializes we can get together on the American soil, to prove any land is good and worthy to impart knowledge from competent teacher to a worthy student.

I am happy to read your letters and I must hand over my robe to you.

Transmit peace and happiness to all beings of this planet, postpone your own Nirvana.

> Talk not about the Truth
> Think not about the Truth
> When No thoughts arise
> You are, what you ARE
>
> *H. W. L. Poonja*

January 3, 1987
Totnes, England

Dear MASTER, My FATHER, My SELF,

This morning your last letter from India arrived. In this letter I am enclosing some letters from my students to you, describing their experiences with me. I sent some also to Haridwar one month ago, I hope that you will receive it eventually in New York. I am planning to leave England for New York to come and see you with Alka around January 25th. Here more and more people are coming all the time. Every evening between twenty-five and forty-five people come for Satsanga. During the day I see people individually. Even though I could easily stay here in England for another three months and remain busy, I feel the call to leave this place, to move on, for a change. I will return here after two months in Holland. Master! My mind reels at all that is taking place around me here. My God, FATHER, you knew all this would happen I know, but so fast, so fast?! This is indeed a difficult life FATHER that I have been chosen for. At times the strain of the power of Maya in the minds of those who come to me disturbs me. At times the thought of great numbers of people coming to me makes me want to run away and hide; to be quiet and alone with only a few who could really give their lives to this JEWEL that you have given me. But then when I see the light and Love that is being realized through YOUR GRACE in those who come to me, it makes it all worth it and I have no doubt for I know I have no choice. My life is no longer my own. It is now only yours MASTER and in that, my Love is only Your own.

I have been learning so much about this mystery FATHER, there is much that I want to share with you, MYSELF who understands so much more than me. I know NOTHING MASTER, NOTHING AT ALL, and it is only the ignorance in those who come to me that creates the illusion that I know something. It is only darkness that makes light visible, but to the light itself, there is only light and NOTHING ELSE. When there is ONLY LIGHT, to whom could darkness exist? In Light there is no darkness and no light, Nothing at all, and THAT cannot be known by a mind that still perceives opposites of any kind. Light only exists for those who live in darkness, but to those to whom there is no darkness there is no light either. There is only NOTHING AT ALL in which EVERYTHING is known.

I look forward to seeing your physical body with anticipation and joy—with the clear understanding that we could never be apart Father, for we never really met each other, we never could have. We have never been separate beloved FATHER, but with that clear understanding, I still shake with Love at the illusion of your face and body. This illusion will never die MASTER, until I die physically. Until that time your body is a Temple to me MASTER, and your Love is that into which I have died, leaving no trace.

I   LOVE   ONLY   YOU

I   LOVE

I

0

Your own true son,

Andrew

March 4, 1987
Hawaii

Dear Andrew,

...You will give me the details of how you have presented the no teaching to Enlighten the people by no way whatsoever. If you can't write ask someone to do it. I send you my Love, and Love to everyone who is around you.

Your own Self

H. W. L. Poonja

April 9, 1987
Amsterdam

Dear Master,

Father, the Mystery continues to unfold timelessly in time, always unknown yet recognized and beheld in endless humility and wonder. Your Grace and Love is daily being showered upon all those who come to me. The effect is staggering for all, as who could ever imagine this Unknown, Unthinkable beauty to be shining so brightly Master here in Europe through your own true son? He cannot imagine it. He accepts it for he has no choice, for his life is now and forever only YOUR own. YOUR will is his will and YOUR Love his Love. He Loves You so dearly that all else has vanished from his memory. He loves only YOU, only YOU only YOU — and in YOU he has lost this world and the universe in which it exists. His world is no world and his face is only your NO FACE where this universe never was and where there is no beginning that needs to be understood. Lost forever in Your Arms Master he is Unborn and therefore has realized NOTHING that can be remembered. In Nothing he is Safe, for in THAT NO-THING there was never anyone to be caught, bound or confused. No confusion in NO memory is Unthought, Unimagined LOVE BLISS that never ever realized anything other than *ITSELF.*

Here for only six weeks Master and so much work being done! Something seems to have happened to your son while sitting at your feet in New York. All the people coming from England have told me that there is a change in me since I have seen You. It must be so, for my effect on those around me here is more powerful than before. OH Master — what have You done?!

Whatever happens Father from now on — I feel safe in NOT KNOWING. I feel protected in a sense by my own innocence. I know I am not the doer in spite of the way it seems and in that I am safe. I am only Your Servant and in that service I know only You. In You I am not and if I am not — there is TRUE FREEDOM and LOVE. UNKNOWN LOVE belongs to NO ONE and LOVES only ITSELF. In that LOVE — how could anyone do anything for any other?

My life here goes on much the same as it did in England. We are living together in a very pleasant apartment. I see people privately during the day and every evening we hold Satsang at an apartment that belongs to one of my students. A steady stream of people from England have been coming and going since my arrival here and about five are staying here in Amsterdam as long as I will be here. The Dutch people have been slow to recognize the truly unheard of nature of what is taking place here. There is a small but growing group of them that are now very much in love with this Beauty that has no history.

I plan to stay here in Amsterdam for another four to six weeks and then we are thinking of going to Israel for one month after which we will return to England. Master like yourself I don't like to be pinned down to fixed plans and very much prefer to leave future plans open. This addiction to not being pinned down I have caught from you no doubt.

Please write to me Father and let me know how you

are and about all that is happening. I think of you always — for you are all that I AM.

ALL   MY   LOVE   FOREVER

Your own true son,

Andrew

May 13, 1987
Haridwar

My dear LOVE,

   Your Love letter passed from hand to hand and finally came to me on the Buddha Purnima day. The day of the Enlightened ONE 2600 years ago. "Buddham saranam gacchami, Buddham saranam gacchami, Buddham saranam gacchami." He is my first teacher at the age of eight years when I lifted in Love with HIM who taught me meditation on emptiness....How Happy I AM to see every one Loves you. Everyone who loves you directly loves me. All those who come and Surrender to you will instantly win **FREEDOM.**

   Love to you. I Love you as I love myself and this my Self is NON*SELF*.

                                    H.W.L. Poonja

September 25, 1987
Totnes, England

Dear Beloved Father,

It's now over five weeks since I left you in Delhi and Father so much has been happening! All this is surely a dream, an unimaginable miracle that never ends! My Father — You are my Beloved SELF. You are always MYSELF and how you have completely taken me in Your Arms and are Loving me so!

Father this MYSTERY never ceases to unfold before me. Your son has become so possessed by this Mystery that is your UNKNOWN FACE that he knows not any longer who he is! He knows only who he imagined himself to be once, a long time ago before the illusion of Andrew had vanished like a mist before YOU. What has *never happened* between us Unknown FATHER is so precious and Beautiful totally beyond the mind's eye to imagine! I LOVE YOU I LOVE YOU I LOVE YOU YOU YOU YOU YOU YOU YOU!

Indeed you have possessed me to such a degree Father — More and More I am melting and dissolving, dying endlessly into Your Unknown LOVE and TRUTH. *Dying Endlessly, Dying endlessly* in YOU is all I AM!

There indeed is a change in your son, Father, since he was near you in Haridwar five weeks ago. You are indeed a Master my Father for at your feet yet again you managed to continue to destroy the last little bits of fear and attachment that I brought to You. When I was with you I could not understand what you were doing with me — why you were keeping me at a distance. Immediately after I left you—at the airport I understood immediately what had happened and why you had to do it. I realized how I had still been depending on you and how in order for me to be able to serve others perfectly I had to be able to stand completely and unconditionally ALONE. You very skillfully cut away my last dependence and the fear that was in its wake. When I left You I realized as never before that this unimaginable Jewel that You have bestowed upon me I must carry ALONE and FREE. Free from all fear and attachment and free from any traces of doubt about my own intuition and surrender. Father I am humbled beyond my words. I stand ALONE as you have shown me that *I must*. There is no longer any desire in me to turn in ANY direction for help. You have given me *Everything* and You are always MYSELF that NEVER LEAVES ME ALONE. YOU ARE MYSELF FOREVER MASTER. YOUR FACE IS MY OWN and I bow before you in silent AWE of your ENDLESS GRACE and INFINITE LOVE. YOU are LOVING ME ALWAYS. YOU NEVER LEAVE ME YOU NEVER LEAVE ME MY LOVE MY LOVE MASTER MASTER!

And so my Father all that you have said would take place before me is happening. On my return from India I spent one week in Amsterdam before returning to England. Every evening that week in Amsterdam the Satsang room was overflowing and two people even came from America to see me for that week. I came back to England on September 4th and Satsang started here again in Devon on September 7th. I am very busy with the work continuously Father. Every evening there is Satsang and between seventy and eighty people are coming. People have gathered here just to be near me and there are several groups of people that have rented houses to stay together during my stay here. I also see people privately every afternoon. I am not busy with this work Father, *but indeed this work is busy with me!* Endlessly absorbed in Your Unknown face I am always learning and discovering more about this MYSTERY Father. Every day it is New and I am overwhelmed each day again and again by the endless depth that is being revealed to me. MASTER YOUR GRACE IS UNIMAGINABLE.

The more work that is taking place Father the more I am learning about this dangerous enemy that MAYA is for so many. The more I teach I am discovering that indeed it is only a rare few who have been born with the rare qualities that give them the strength and innocence with which to fight her powers of deception!

Father what a play this life is! What a dance, what a mystery!

Recently several well-known western meditation teachers came to visit me and yet again I was shocked by how little they know about this Mystery that you have revealed to me my Father. They did not have any idea of this unknown secret that you have bestowed upon me. Many are talking about me and the news is traveling in All directions.

My MASTER your wishes are coming true and you are gaining many Grandchildren FATHER!

I plan to stay here in England for about two and a half more months. A man who came from America to see me in Amsterdam said he would plan a trip for me in America if I wished. When he said this I smiled to myself seeing once again how all your wishes were being fulfilled! How all you have said would happen is happening!

All my love to All those who are gathered around you FATHER.

MY LOVE IS ONLY FOR
YOU MY FATHER — I
THANK YOU + LOVE YOU
ENDLESSLY.
MY LIFE INDEED IS
YOURS

YOUR OWN TRUE SON
Andrew

October 30, 1987
Lucknow, India

Dear Andrew,

Long ago I had received your letter dated 25th September. Many an attempt had been made to reply this only letter remained unreplied among 100 odd letters that have been received and you know my habit of quick responses to every letter by myself. I very much liked to reply back the letter from my only SON but my mind doesn't count you like others who will be satisfied by my Ink and Paper and words. You have so mischievously invaded unto my BE-ing that now I don't discriminate the separate identity of BEingness of even BE-ing.

Never mind—all is going on Beautifully and I am Happy.

All the Love

Your own Self

H. W. L. Poonja

April 13, 1988
Amherst, Massachusetts

Beloved Holy Father,

There is absolutely no doubt that a true revolution in consciousness is exploding here in the west around your own true son. The speed and power of this explosion is impossible for the mind to comprehend. Father it is only now that the true magnitude of this historic event is beginning to dawn on me! Oh Master! TRUTH is such a RARE JEWEL in this barren world! Master what has happened between us has started a raging fire — all of my students are burning with this fire of Love and Truth. A revolution has truly begun! I am speechless before you — all of this you knew from the beginning! Oh Master, who could ever believe that such a Holy fire could rage in the Hearts of so many? My Father the unknown Love is consuming many, many people and all have only one desire — to stay together and abide as one in this Unknown mystery where all appearances dissolve.

I arrived here in America on the 7th of March and have been holding Satsanga each evening for about one month now. The word is spreading fast. Some have come from places like California, Washington and Canada to see me. At the beginning of May, my students from Europe will begin to arrive. I expect over a hundred people to come from Europe over the coming summer months. Many are planning to stay for six months — even those who have families are coming with their children.

The supreme power, *Your Will,* has consumed your son totally Father. He teaches and preaches only one thing—"ENLIGHTENMENT, ENLIGHTENMENT, ENLIGHTENMENT HERE AND NOW." Nothing else Father nothing else. Only absolute Freedom from the known, Freedom from time and all the creations of a fictitious mind and ego.

MASTER I LOVE YOU SO!

My each breath is only YOU and YOU and YOU!

During the last two months and increasing in intensity over the last ten days I have been aware of the fact that I am dying more and more. As my name and fame continue to grow I feel more and more distant. The knowledge of who I am and what I am doing becomes less and less clear. I feel with each passing day that I am becoming more transparent and more distant. I feel less and less connected to this world Father—I feel that I am looking at this existence from a place that is far, far away. This detachment, this distance is growing as my fame grows. The more famous the teacher becomes, the smaller Andrew grows. The more Andrew is known, the less Andrew knows. A strange life this is Father! What an unthinkable destiny you have given me!

Father I love you infinitely and abide only with you and in you. My Love for you is my only reference point.

It is you alone whom I am with on this journey and it is to your feet alone that I cling. All else is **UNREAL**.

Your Servant,

Andrew

P.S. I am living in a wonderful big house in the country with Alka and five others. I will send you pictures.

PLEASE WRITE!

May 6, 1988
Haridwar

Dear Andrew,

Your letter dated April 13th had been received a few days ago. All other letters that I received day after day had been instantly cleared save your letter. Each day I attempted to write but no words poured down from my memory to scribe on the paper. This is because of too much nearness as if Self addressing the SELF. You are seated at the SOURCE, from where the sound emerges to become a word. I am very Happy to learn what is going on and most Happy to see who is at the back of all this phenomenon keeping still and unconcerned. You will yet be surprised what is in store. Andrew + ME will witness this Drama in a near future.

With Love to you, dear Alka and all others,

H. W. L. Poonja

August 18, 1988
Amherst, Massachusetts

Dear Beloved Father,

I am thinking of You and talking to You everyday my most Beloved Father. I am talking to you about this MYSTERY in which you have drowned me. In the past few weeks I have felt this dialogue going on between us, even though I cannot understand the language in which we are speaking! MY Father I love You so! YOU are my Passion, My own Heart. Your Kiss killed me with its unbearable sweetness and your loving embrace holds me safe and free, secure in your arms.

All of THAT which is unfolding around your own true son is without a doubt absolutely KNOWN by Father and son. There is no mistake, no accident and no doubt. This FACT simply IS. My Infinite Father this unbearable Holiness is the most powerful weapon in the universe. It is unstoppable. This FACT is unavoidable. In light of this truth — ALL MUST BE DESTROYED. It has become clear to me that my one and only mission is to destroy absolutely. This LOVE that you have given me is my sword. You have sent me away from You with this one instruction and it is this FACT that has been revealing itself to me again and again and again. This responsibility is unbearable for the mind to even consider, but there is *NO CHOICE*. Having NO CHOICE I must *ACT*.

ALL MUST BE DESTROYED!

At this time, many people are coming each evening for Satsanga. About one hundred are here from Europe. Three quarters of the people are giving up everything to follow me. I have not asked them to do so. They are all feeling compelled to follow me. I realize that is my one and only duty to my Master that I must most perfectly NOT RESIST this explosion and simply allow this unthinkable Holy Drama to unfold as it will. I prostrate to YOU my Father again and again and again.

We are moving to Boston at the end of this month and I plan to stay there for about four months.

By this time people have heard about me all over America. Within six months or one year I cannot imagine what will be happening. This message, this Teaching, this SECRET has been lost in TIME and is now being revealed to all those who would be willing to accept it *here* and *now*.

OH MASTER IT'S ALL TOO MUCH TO BEAR AND YET THERE IS NOTHING ELSE TO DO— I LOVE YOU I LOVE YOU I LOVE YOU.

Your own True son,

Andrew

January 8, 1989
Cambridge, Massachusetts

Dear Beloved Father,

After leaving India on November 18th, Alka and I flew to England where we spent ten days. My students there organized one week of Satsang to be held for seven consecutive evenings. Over two hundred people came, many from different parts of Europe. The photos I have sent you are from this week. We arrived back in Boston at the end of November. The last month has been very busy with Satsang five nights a week and a lot of work being done on the two books that I told you about when I was with you in Lucknow. The first book will consist mainly of the diary that I kept during my initial meeting with you in 1986 and will also include the letters that we have written to each other over the past two and a half years. We are writing an outline to the story of our meeting and of how the teaching began in Rishikesh spontaneously through your Grace.

The Mystery of *YOUR GRACE* Father, is really what this book will be about. Also through our correspondence it shows in a very rare way the Unbearable LOVE between Father and son. The meaning of SURRENDER and of LOVE for the MASTER.

MY FATHER I LOVE YOU!

The second book will consist of transcriptions from the evening Satsangs and copies of letters I have received from my students describing their experiences....This is what we are working on now. It is fantastic Father because it was you who told me that I would write a book — You told me this after you had a dream about it over one and a half years ago!

What is happening around me, my Father, through YOUR GRACE — is too fantastic and too beautiful for words. A real SANGHA is growing around me and many of my students are catching my FIRE. There are now twenty houses here in Cambridge where my students are living together. Many have come from Europe and are staying for long periods. This decision to live together and come together to be near me has happened quite spontaneously and naturally. I have not told anyone to do so, but this is their wish. As this has been happening steadily by itself over the last year and a half, a real Sangha is being born. The teaching is ENLIGHTENMENT and the teacher speaks of nothing else. The living understanding of this living truth is being lived by many of my students, and it is only through YOUR GRACE that this is happening.

As each day passes Father I feel my strength and confidence growing stronger and stronger. You told me how truly rare this event is, but it has taken two years for me to understand what you were saying. I could not believe you as it simply seemed *too much to believe*. But now Father, I not only believe but I *KNOW* it's true. And this fact is unbearable and terrifying. But I am not terrified Father. Simply I know, and in this I am at Rest. That which cannot be borne is borne and there is no conflict and no fear. It is all only your Love and GRACE and I simply am not interfering with what feels pre-planned and perfect. Oh my Father with each day my recognition of the mission you have given me deepens and with it I feel more and more fire and zeal which is my fuel. The desire that "this living truth must be known" burns within me Father and yet I know fully well that this is not my desire at all but your own. Because the real mystery of it all is that as my fire increases and confidence grows, my own sense of Freedom and detachment also increases. This really means that as I become more sure, I simultaneously know less about what I am doing or how I am doing it. What a Mystery Father. Who are You who is the source and cause of all this? Who are You, my Master? It is my Love and surrender to You alone, You who does *not exist* that I survive.

On my knees before You Father,

I LOVE ONLY YOU,

Your Servant and True Son,

Andrew

February 1, 1989
Lucknow

Very dearly dear Son,

   Received your loving letter each word entered my bones and shakes up my body So Happy I always feel whenever I receive news about you and hear from people who come to see me. Some of them have heard of you, even as far as far east and even entire Europe and Latin America. They will go to Cambridge to see you.

   What is going on around you is a miracle. You are a gifted person. All my 75 years I could get a serious, sincere, dedicated, obedient disciple who moved so close to my Heart Soul and body. Whenever I move I feel I speak through your mouth and live in your body.

   My Love to you. All my children live happy and peaceful life.

H. W. L. Poonja

March 25, 1989
Cambridge, Massachusetts

Beloved Father,

Today is our anniversary. Three years ago I met you. I can never thank you for the infinite grace you have bestowed upon me. You have set me Free. Andrew died when he met you. He who lives in his name is now only your reflection. I love you and thank you endlessly.

Andrew

Addendum

The extraordinary love story recounted in this book was the end of seeking for Andrew Cohen. But time would reveal that it was only the beginning of his recognition of the meaning and significance of Enlightenment.

The bond between these two unusual people eventually fell apart. The issues that led to the dissolution of their relationship are many and complex. The very nature of spiritual awakening was brought into question through a painful unfolding of a conflict that revealed the entire panorama of important questions that need to be addressed by any individual who sincerely wants to be free in this life. The story is told in Andrew's later work *Autobiography of an Awakening.*

Largely as a result of the original publication of this work, H.W.L. Poonja became within two years one of the most sought-after gurus in India. Andrew's following gradually grew into a worldwide community of students with centers in the United States, England, Holland, Germany and Israel. Since the original publication of this book, his teaching has continued to evolve in dramatic ways and has over time become an original expression of a complete teaching that embraces both heaven and earth. He has recently published his fourth book *An Unconditional Relationship to Life.*

GLOSSARY

Karma: Law of cause and effect.

Maya: Illusion, the way things appear to be.

Nirvana: The bliss of the Realization of Liberation.

Pranam: Greeting showing deep respect.

Rishi: Sage or wise man.

Ramana Maharshi (1879-1950): Renowned and venerated spiritual Teacher who lived in South India.

Satguru: Spiritual Teacher who is at one with Truth or SELF.

Samadhi: The joy of Self Knowledge.

Samsara: The illusion of separate existence.

Sangha: Spiritual community.

Satsang(a): Association with Truth, being in the presence of a Satguru.

Vedas: Hindu Scriptures.

I would like to thank Bradley Roth and Amy Edelstein for all their help in compiling and editing the manuscript. I would also like to thank Judy Fox for her assistance in the production of this book.

A. C.

For information about
Andrew Cohen and his teachings:

MOKSHA FOUNDATION
P.O. Box 5265
Larkspur, CA 94977
USA
tel: 415-927-3210
fax: 415-927-2032

FACE CENTRE
(Friends of Andrew Cohen in Europe)
Centre Studios
Englands Lane
London NW3 4YD
UK
tel: 44-171-483-3732
fax: 44-171-916-3170